Defeating an Internet Boogeyman:
Simple Secrets of Reputation & Crisis
Management Using Social Media &
Web Marketing Strategy

Mason Duchatschek, Adam Burns, Will Hanke

Foreword

Over the years, business owners have been taught (by advertisers) that if they spent enough on advertising, their prospects would remember THEIR names, THEIR products and THEIR services when they were ready to buy. The whole goal was to create top of the mind awareness for their products and services.

Things were simple back then. Consumers would recognize a need, remember a name, open up the yellow pages and buy stuff.

Times have changed. Many consumers take advantage of an optional step to the buying process. It's called Internet research and almost everybody who has access to a mobile phone, tablet or computer goes online to do research before they make a purchase.

Consumers search. They compare. They contrast. They read reviews. They watch videos. They also DISCUSS and

SHARE their opinions, thoughts and experiences about products, services and companies they buy from with others online.

Research shows that consumers also place SIGNIFI-CANTLY more TRUST in what they see and hear in reviews and discussions online than in what they are shown in advertisements.

So.... what's your plan when (not if):

1. An employee doesn't follow policy or training and says or does something to a customer that they shouldn't have, and the customer goes online to tell anyone who will listen how awful your company is to work with?

2. A competitor PRETENDS to be a mistreated past customer and blasts you, your products and your services so effectively online that the sales leads you spent YOUR advertising dollars to generate RUN the other way?

How do you make it go away? Simply spending more on advertising will assure that MORE of your ideal prospects are going to see the awful things being said about you.

The good news is that the authors of this book have the answers, and you no longer have to accept the consequences of lost sales opportunities, public humiliation and personal embarrassment forever. You and your business do not need to remain a hostage to an "Internet Boogeyman" who seeks to destroy the reputation and branding you've worked so hard and so long to build.

This book is a step by step, blueprint and action plan showing you how to repair, build and protect your valuable brand and reputation online, even if you're not a techie. It is full of simple, basic and fundamental tips, strategies and tools that every business owner needs to implement right now, or pay dearly later.

Shep Hyken, Customer Service Expert
The New York Times best-selling author

Welcome

IS THIS BOOK FOR YOU?

With few exceptions, consumers go online to do research before making a purchase locally. If all they see when they find you or your company is criticism, complaints and horror stories, even if they're not true, it could mean you're screwed.

It doesn't have to!

Don't want your business destroyed by angry past customers or jealous competitors POSING as angry past customers and saying horrible things about you online?

Need to neutralize and minimize the damage being done to your reputation right now because you're already under attack?

Online reputation management, when implemented correctly with a step-by-step plan, can help your business repair, build and preserve the value of your name and brand online. This book shows you how.

WHAT'S IN THE BOOK?

This is a simple (not overly technical) book focused on web marketing strategy and social media marketing secrets. It offers entrepreneurs and managers easy-to-follow strategies and detailed blueprints to help resurrect and protect reputations online.

It's a quick read containing real-world examples, helpful and practical tips.

WHAT'S IN IT FOR YOU?

Peace of Mind.

We know business owners who suffer from sleepless nights because they were so consumed with worry about the damage caused by an Internet Boogeyman. Because they had no idea what (if anything) they could do about it, there was no relief for their anxiety, fear or hopelessness.

Your biggest takeaway is probably going to be the serenity that happens when you are prepared to deal with almost anything a current or future Internet Boogeymen could throw at you. Even if you aren't a "techie" or expert at web marketing strategy, there are some fundamental tools you can do to protect everything you've worked for.

In summary, you will discover:

1. Where and how an Internet Boogeyman is most likely to attack your reputation online (so you can prepare to counter their moves in advance.)

2. How to set up an "early warning monitoring system" that automatically lets you know when people are talking about you online (so you can quickly respond and turn problems into opportunities.)

3. How to use social media for business and generate new leads and customers (so you can supercharge your marketing opportunities including Facebook, Twitter, YouTube, Pinterest and LinkedIn.)

4. How to build a "virtual force-field" around your name and reputation online (so damaging content posted by an Internet Boogeyman gets bounced so far down search engine result pages that hardly anyone will ever see them.)

5. The secrets of creating "search engine friendly" content in different formats (blogs, articles, videos, podcasts, social media posts, etc.) so your prospects find YOUR reasons to buy instead of an Internet Boogeyman's reasons why they shouldn't.

6. How your advertising budget can be used against you (so you can prevent competitors from siphoning away YOUR business leads without your knowledge.)

7. The best social media and online marketing tools for automating and replacing the time consuming "grunt work" (so YOU get an unfair advantage over your online adversaries.)

8. The most common "knee-jerk" tactics and strategies that hurt more than they help (and why you should avoid them, even if they sound tempting.)

Chapter 1 - The Power of the Internet Boogeyman

Who is the Internet Boogeyman?

The Internet Boogeyman can be anyone. It can be a current employee with a grudge. It can be a past employee who has an axe to grind. It can be an angry customer who felt mistreated / disrespected/ripped off and wants to get even by preventing others from having the same kind of perceived experience. It can be a bored internet expert who randomly picked you because it is "fun" to ruin others. It can be a competitor who wants to sabotage your business or steal your customers.

Why You MUST Protect or Restore Your Good Reputation Online!

If you and your business haven't been targeted yet, it doesn't mean it won't happen. How you prepare in advance to handle a potential situation can make or break your personal and business reputation for years to come.

The ideas in this tactical book comprise remedies that are intended to help approximately 95-99% of all businesses seeking to prevent or minimize damage caused by Internet Boogeymen.

We tried to avoid getting into overly technical terms and issues that regular people, business owners and "non-techies" might have challenges grasping or implementing. We tried to keep things simple.

You don't need to understand everything to apply the information. You don't need to implement EVERYTHING we tell you to protect or repair your online reputation. However, keep this in mind: the more you do and the more consistently you do it, the better you'll get at it and the more you will benefit.

Picking Sides?

We wrote this book from a non-judgmental perspective. It's not our place to speculate whether you or your business "deserves" the wrath of an Internet Boogeyman.

Nobody is perfect. People make mistakes. Employees say and do things that do NOT reflect the policies or training they have been given. Regardless, the business owner can STILL be held responsible long after those employees have moved on.

Our purpose in writing this book is to help you recognize the potential damage that can be caused by an Internet Boogeyman. Our goal is to give you the knowledge, tools and strategies to prevent it, minimize it, recover from it and maybe even use it to your advantage by making you and your business processes better and more customer-focused as a result.

Encounters With an Internet Boogeyman

What do encounters with an Internet Boogeyman look like?

What are the repercussions?

What are the costs of inaction?

What are the costs of the WRONG actions?

What ONLINE and OFFLINE options and strategies are best suited for your unique situation?

Let's explore them together...

A Drunken Frat Boy Mistake

The Problem:

We got a call one day from a young man who was finding it impossible to get a good job. He was having relationship issues too. There was one BIG problem, and he didn't know how to solve it.

He had a college degree and, based on his transcripts, it looked like he was not only smart but also active on campus. What was his problem?

Good kids do dumb stuff. It happens. It's part of growing up. In his case, he was in a fraternity, drank too much one night, had issues with his prescription drugs, and got out of control. A young lady accused him of instigating an altercation with her.

He couldn't tell us about the altercation because he didn't remember it. He blacked out. Unfortunately for him, the police report ... and the campus newspaper ... and the local media filled everything in for him ... plus the rest of the world ... thanks to the Internet.

He apologized and made amends with the young lady. He had no record of violent, abusive or unlawful behavior before or after that one night. He accepted responsibility and, to this day, insists that he is not the person who behaved that way and is infinitely embarrassed, humiliated and mortified by his behavior.

Years later - long after the matter had been resolved, NO CHARGES were filed and his name had been CLEARED - his nightmare remained. Because of the media's interest, there were links to the story, as well as comments and discussions showcased online...and there was nothing he could do to undo the situation.

The Repercussions:

Anytime a potential employer typed his name in Google as part of a background check, the story came up. He invested four years of his life and tens of thousands of dollars for an education he is still trying to pay for ... but can't without a good job. Keeping a girlfriend past "The Google Search" also has proven impossible.

Name = Brand = Mud

The Problem:

We know of a car dealer who spends hundreds of thousands of dollars per year in radio and TV advertising in just one metropolitan market. He has GREAT name recognition. That's part of the problem.

His non-stop advertising works because you can't forget his name, the type of cars he sells and where he sells them. That's not necessarily a good thing. Here's why.

He IS his brand. Lets call him "Joe Blow" and pretend his dealerships are in the fictitious city of Anytown. Let's do this for the sake of discussion since he's truly getting destroyed online in the real world, and we aren't ones to pile it on.

When we type the actual equivalent of "Joe Blow Anytown" (his name and the city he works in), the first page of Google is plastered with terrible reviews and hater sites built by SEVERAL Internet Boogeymen who clearly want to cause damage to his brand and cost him future leads.

We are looking at it right now. The first listing on the page is "Joe Blow's" website. The second and third listings are two star reviews (out of a possible five) appearing on Yelp.com and Cars.com. The fourth listing on the first Google page is a site called the equivalent of "MyJoeBlowCarSucks.com" which, upon further investigation, describes IN DETAIL how one customer was "ripped off" … plus it serves as a forum for those who have been "ripped off" to tell their stories too! The seventh and eighth listings on the first page are Better Business Bureau reviews and complaints directed at several of his different dealerships.

Repercussions:

He is SQUANDERING a HUGE percentage of his own advertising budget. He also is paying money to spread the information that further DAMAGES his OWN reputation while driving away more of the exact same people who he is trying to target.

When people looking to buy a car remember his name and then search online to find his contact information, they're going to see the "Internet Herpes" this guy has created from screwing the wrong people and turning them into Internet Boogeymen. They are NOT going to do business with his dealership when they read the ugly details revealed online.

Hidden Camera Extortion: News "Creation" Covered By Free Speech

The Problem:

Not long ago, a KSDK Channel 5 reporter went into a suburban public high school in Kirkwood, a town just outside of St. Louis. The reporter left the school's office and walked down the halls without permission, prompting an all-out security lockdown at the high school and unnecessarily striking fear in both parents and students. The reporter claimed he was doing an investigative report on school security.

In short, he created a story. He made news so he could report on it. Why? To get attention? To be a hero? Who knows.

Well, guess what? In this day and age of high definition cell phone cameras and dash cameras ANYBODY can call himself a citizen journalist. ANYONE can observe, report or CREATE news. Anyone can play "gotcha" with a camera and put embarrassing, harmful footage online for the world to see. There is more to worry about now than just television reporters.

Some want revenge. Some want fame. Some are bored and are wreaking havoc for their own entertainment. Others want money.

Just like the news reporter at KSDK Channel 5 was able to CREATE a story, an Internet Boogeyman can too. And, an Internet Boogeyman can use that story to cause lots of damage.

We've heard stories of Internet Boogeyman who try to extort businesses with hidden camera footage of their work that is "edited" to look as though the consumer did something wrong. When the business owner is confronted by the Internet Boogeymen, he is given a choice: either pay or let the "created news" ruin his reputation online.

Repercussions:

Should the owner sue the "customer" and risk drawing more negative attention to his business? Could he even win a battle in court or is the Internet Boogeyman's edited "handiwork" protected by free speech? Would he look like a bully picking on a "helpless victim" in the court of public opinion even though he really didn't do anything wrong? Is the business owner relegated to picking the least negative path since none of the options are good?

What options exist? Which ones are best? Why?

I Won... But Lost:

The Problem:

A businessman got involved in a lawsuit more than 10 years ago, and the charges made him sound like a crook. The stories were in the local media. He won the lawsuit and, if people took the time to read through the details of the case (more than 20 pages), he looked just fine.

Unfortunately, his name showed up in search engines associated with negative and disparaging headlines while the truth was buried in long, boring documents that nobody took the time to read.

Repercussions:

He is missing out on deals, relationships and opportunities that he would otherwise be profiting from.

Competitors Who Fuel the Fire/Can't Erase the Internet

The Problem:

A car owner without warranty coverage walked into a specialty transmission repair shop complaining about transmission problems. After multiple visits and more than $1,500 in repair bills, he claimed his car was still making a funny sound.

So, he goes back to the dealer where he bought his car. He tells them the story about the funny noise and how the transmission place didn't fix the problem. The car dealer added fuel to this man's fire and - rather than suggest that the car was safe to operate or that the sound might not have had anything to do with the transmission - turned him into the Internet Boogeyman with his venom placed solely at the specialty transmission shop.

For the sake of discussion, let's call it "Transmission Shop X" and pretend it is in a city called Anytown. Today when we went to Google and typed in the transmission shop's name and town it's REALLY located in, here's what we found on the first page of Google: the first listing is the company's website. The second listing says, in big bold letters "BEWARE of Transmission Shop X in Anytown." The fifth listing (still on the first page) says "Transmission Shop X is a ripoff - Anytown, - Pissed Consumer."

Here's the kicker. We actually KNOW the business owner. He did sue this Internet Boogeyman … and he won. The case took place several years ago. The damaging posts and sites were supposed to be taken down. We are looking at them right now, and YEARS have passed. There is definitely no erase button on the Internet.

Repercussions:

This business owner has spent a fortune - literally - on radio, television, print and other traditional advertising to get consumers to remember his company name. He paid expensive legal bills to fight the Internet Boogeyman. He invested countless hours battling this "hater" that should have been invested in building his business. The Internet Boogeyman's "handiwork" smear campaign is still on display for all his potential clients to see.

People rely on their phones, tablets and computers to search online for a company's phone number, address and hours of operation. This owner has a HUGE obstacle that has FIRMLY lodged itself between the moment a potential client remembers his company name and the point where they actually come in and purchase his services.

That wall - the one that stands between the point of name recognition and the time a purchase occurs - is thick and tall. He can't advertise his current problem away. Advertising only helps with name recognition, not the obstacle that happens after it.

Business Couldn't Be Better (But It REALLY Could):

The Problem:

There is a hair transplant doctor who advertises like crazy in his metro area. If you lived in that same market, it is very likely that you would know his name.

You can easily figure that he invests more than $500,000 each year in radio and television advertising to make sure people know his name and what he does. You can also be lead to believe that the doctor's sales and marketing manager doesn't see the value in marketing online because they have "enough" patients and are profitable. They credit their advertising as the reason.

Business couldn't be better. Or could it?

In his mind, the doctor has no reason to worry. He just needs to work on hair restoration. He hired a manager to market his business. And he has enough new patients to earn a decent living.

The marketing manager has a vested interest in the status quo and doesn't want the boss to hear about any bad news. His radio and television advertisements actually direct people to their website to learn more.

We just typed this specific doctor's name in Google and here's what came up today. The first page's first listing is their website. The second listing REALLY stood out from the rest. Why? Because it was a video and a DISGUSTING picture of a person with what is known as NECROSIS of the scalp.

Don't do this if you have a weak stomach. It is GROSS to see. If you think you can handle it, go to Google and type in "NECROSIS". Select "Images" from the Google "Search Tools" options right near the search bar to see all the pictures.

According to Wikipedia, necrosis is "the death of most or all of the cells in an organ or tissue due to disease, injury, or failure of the blood supply." It appears the work performed by this doctor and his staff destroyed a man's scalp and created an Internet Boogeyman. Before and after pictures were taken to create a YouTube video that ranks second on Google's first page when the doctor's name is searched.

On Google's fourth listing on the first page, the Internet Boogeyman created a site with the doctor's name followed by a dash and the word "NIGHTMARE" in the url/domain name. He told the story of how he spent more than $10,000 for a procedure that got messed up and had graphic proof that was strong enough to turn stomachs ... and send potential clients running.

Repercussions:

Some business owners don't understand the Internet's effect on their business and online marketing. They don't take action since they aren't sure how to determine return on their investment. Just because they don't know how to calculate one, it doesn't mean there isn't one.

What this particular doctor SHOULD be paying attention to is the OPPORTUNITY cost of inaction. At this time, the YouTube video has been active for about two years. The current view count is 1,892. At approximately $10,000 per procedure, we are talking about LOST BUSINESS revenue amounting to more than $18 million over the last two years or $9 million PER year on an annual basis!

Even if half of them could afford it by using a financing plan, that's a $4.5 MILLION PER YEAR problem. If the video continues for 10 years, we are still talking about a $45 MILLION problem that isn't going away by itself!

Think about it. The people who type this doctor's name into Google probably heard or saw an ad, recognized their need, and then took the time to investigate because they wanted a hair loss solution. They were MOTIVATED potential buyers willing to take action! Many were probably inspired to find a way to pay for this procedure even if they couldn't afford it.

Chapter 2 - Building a Force Field Around Your Business

To date, our professional experience shows fewer than eight out of 10 people who perform an Internet search never look past the first page of search engine results. What this means: if you can get YOUR content to take over the first page of the search engine results, you **have** solved 80-90% of your problem.

That's the goal of reputation restoration, protection, and damage control. Bury and "push down" harmful content produced by an Internet Boogeyman and replace it with the positive content YOU create.

Likely Targets

When preparing for battle, young military officers are taught to analyze their enemy's most desirable "high value" targets so they can devise a plan to defend them. The three most popular and likely targets of an Internet Boogeyman are:

1. Your Name
2. Your Company Name
3. Your Products / Reviews

Likely Avenues of Approach

Young military officers are also taught to analyze their enemy's most likely avenues of approach. Previous ways to spread ideas included direct mail, billboards, radio, television, newspapers and magazines.

Today online message delivery mechanisms are growing in popularity. They exist as websites, blogs, podcast channels, video channels and social media sites (also known as "status sites") that update friends, fans and followers about what's going on in a real-time basis.

Most Internet Boogeymen don't have a budget to buy television or radio ads. They realize the impact fades shortly after the ad runs.

Because they are free, they use the multi-million dollar distribution platforms that companies like Facebook, Twitter, YouTube and others have set up for spreading their message!

Monitoring/Alerts

What's your Boogeyman up to? How can you monitor his activity in order to immediately respond? How can you be most aware of the online community as it relates to you without spending a ton of time or money?

The best answer, in our opinion, is neither expensive nor time consuming. You can set it up all by yourself in a matter of minutes. Here's how.

Go to http://www.Google.com/alerts. As of the date of this publication, you can get Google to scan the latest and most relevant search results for any word or phrase YOU designate. And it's FREE.

First enter a word or phrase that you want Google to monitor in the "Search Query" box. Next select what type of results you want Google to gather. Your choices include the following: Everything, News, Blogs, Video, Discussions, and Books.

You then have the option to choose the content's "Language" and the "Country" the content is originating in. This can be important if you handle international business.

Google Alerts will then ask how often you want the results sent to you (usually via email). Your choices are "As it happens", "Once a day" or "Once a week."

Your final step before pressing the button to create the Google Alert: specify how many results you want to receive.

Your options include "Only the best results" (as determined by Google) and "All results."

Google Alerts should be set up to monitor (at a minimum) your name, company name, product and service names, and some of your most important keyword phrases that are directly tied to the local markets you serve. To run an alert on a competitor's website, type **site:**www.domain.com (using their website address, of course). This will alert you every time a competitor adds or updates a page on their site.

If you want to monitor and respond to mentions and direct messages through your most popular social media channels from one place, then there also are inexpensive options. We happen to be a fan of http://www.hootsuite.com.

The Foundation of Your Defense Online: Keyword Research

Keyword research is the foundation of what will eventually become the force-field protecting you from both direct and indirect online attacks aimed at you and your business. Once you PROPERLY identify your keyword phrases, then they must get embedded into all future content (titles, tags, descriptions, etc.) that you create and distribute to a variety of Internet sites.

Why do you need to create content in so many forms (articles, blogs, websites, podcasts, etc.)? Why do you need to know what keywords to include in your content? Why does your content need to get distributed to so many places?

The answer is two-fold. First, you need to have your content appearing in social media and search engine results for your name, company name, product/service names, and the keyword phrases that are valuable to your business. The reason: online is WHERE YOUR PROSPECTS are. You want customers to find YOUR content INSTEAD of the Internet Boogeyman's.

Second, if your online presence is confined to only one website, then you will likely get ONE listing on the first page of search engine results. What about the rest? You need to have as many listings on the first page of search results as you can so YOUR content is found during online searches instead of the ideas created by an Internet Boogeyman.

You and your business are vulnerable to a variety of devastating online attacks. Some attacks are direct; others are designed to indirectly destroy your name and business right under your nose while remaining hidden in plain sight. Make sure to recognize potential damage and prepare for the worst case scenario.

Direct Attacks

Usually when an Internet Boogeyman goes after your name, it is obvious. When you type your name in a search engine and see an Internet Boogeyman sharing his hate, he wants you to see it. It was created to embarrass, humiliate you and harm your ability to do business.

Try typing your company name or some of your most popular (and profitable) products and/or services in a search engine. If you see an Internet Boogeyman giving bad reviews, creating blogs, videos and websites to "tell the world" about how much they despise your company, then they want you (and everyone else) to see it.

Indirect Attacks

The REALLY sneaky ones may NOT be angry past customers. They might be web-savvy competitors who want to redirect leads to their business that YOU paid for with YOUR advertising dollars.

In our book "Attract, Capture & Convert: 89 Simple Ways Entrepreneurs Make Money Online (& Offline) Using Social Media & Web Marketing Strategy" (see http://www.AttractCaptureConvertBook.com), we talked about how your competitors can use your very own advertising budget against you.

Fortunately most of your competitors aren't going to be this shrewd. Others won't have the guts to risk your eventually finding out. The rest either don't care what you think or don't believe you're smart enough to catch them. An Internet Boogeyman can be ruthless in trying to outsmart you, especially if he thinks it can happen without being caught.

When agencies try to sell you their advertising services to promote your business, what do they claim is one of your biggest objectives? It's to create top of mind awareness ... right? Isn't the goal to get ideal prospects to remember your company name or products when they recognize a need and are ready to buy?

Here's what advertising agencies don't tell you. And it has a lot to do with consumer behavior.

What often happens right AFTER a potential customer recognizes a need or desire for your product or service and BEFORE they actually visit your business? The answer: they do research online.

Since it is only getting easier to do research online thanks to Internet-connected mobile phones (which almost everyone has), tablets and computers, we don't see the trend reversing anytime soon. It's a mobile society. People don't carry the Yellow Pages everywhere they go.

Their "research" may be as simple as typing your product or company name into a search engine along with your city's name. Why? They might just want to call and find out your address or hours of operation. Maybe they don't want to make the drive and find out you are closed that day? They also may want to know if you have a specific product in stock before they make the trip?

On the other hand, maybe they want to read reviews and compare your offerings with other choices available to them. They want to know the best price. They want warranty information. They want to know how your products stack up against the competition.

If an Internet Boogeyman knows how to get favorable information about THEIR products and services to appear in search engine results for YOUR company, product or service names, then THEY can funnel valuable leads (and sales revenue) that YOU paid for directly to themselves.

For example, let's pretend you are BRAND X and assume you "effectively" advertise and have great name recognition. Let's pretend that plenty of your ideal customers are typing your company and product names into search engines when they recognize a need.

For the sake of discussion, we can assume that you have a BRAND X website to promote your business and it is likely to come up on the first page of search engine results. Here is our question: What about all the OTHER listings on the same search page results? What if the rest of the listings were tied to content (websites, videos, blogs, articles, podcasts, etc.) created by an Internet Boogeyman?

What if the Internet Boogeyman created multiple videos, blogs, websites or podcasts comparing advantages and disadvantages of your BRAND X product A, B, or C to HIS company's product A, B, or C?

What if there were alternative websites listed that the Internet Boogeyman owned and managed, calling them something like BRANDXREVIEWS.COM? What about social media posts or podcasts TIED TO HIS company accounts that mentioned your BRAND X items and contained discussions around product pros and cons, as well as LINKS TO ALTERNATIVE products like his?

This is an aggressive strategy because it allows an Internet Boogeyman to surround all your products, services and stores ONLINE. Once the Internet Boogeyman has claimed the virtual real estate around your best products, services and location searches online, it becomes a huge asset for him and a big drain on your profits. It's so effective since, before prospects can get to YOU, they have to be able to get around, avoid or ignore the work done by the Internet Boogeyman.

While there are still freedoms of speech and the press in the United States, it would be difficult to make a case that it is illegal to criticize, review, or discuss your brands and products. This basically means that Internet Boogeymen have a vast playground and few limits on what they can or will do.

Wal-Mart has deep pockets and access to some of the world's best attorneys. If they can't shut down WalmartSucks.org (which has been in existence for more than 13 years), then good luck if you think you can shut down an Internet Boogeyman who is simply trying to compare and contrast your products and services with theirs.

The Primary Components of Keyword Research

In addition to protecting your name and your company in the cities where you do business, it is CRITICAL that you KNOW (don't guess or assume) what OTHER words and keyword phrases your ideal customers are entering into search engines when they are ready to research or buy your products or services.

It is a HUGE (but common) mistake to sit around a table with family members, co-workers or friends and ask what they THINK current and potential customers are entering into search engines to get information about you and your business.

The good news for you: most, but not all, Internet Boogeymen make the same mistake. If you avoid this mistake - which includes performing proper keyword research, creating lots of content using the right keyword phrases, and distributing content in various forms and sites (podcasts, articles, blogs, videos, etc.) - then you have a HUGE advantage over most Internet Boogeymen.

Traffic

People type potential words or keyword phrases into search engines every day. You need to uncover these since it doesn't help to create a bunch of content that ranks on the first page of search engines when few, if any, of your ideal prospects are typing them in.

Let the Internet Boogeymen waste their time, talent and energy creating content that isn't going to get found by anyone ... or anyone that matters to you. That's exactly what happens when they embed those same (unsearched) phrases into their work. They don't know which words or phrases your ideal prospects are typing into search engines in any significant numbers.

YOU need to know what words or phrases your ideal prospects and customers are mainly typing into search engines so you can make sure you create (and distribute) web content in lots of forms (articles, videos, podcasts, blogs, etc.) to all kinds of important sites.

Competition

You and your business crave space on the first page of search engine results. Not only are you competing with current or potential Internet Boogeymen, but you also are contending with other real businesses trying to get those high rankings.

What if you could know in advance the chances that your content might actually appear on the first page of search engine results BEFORE you spent the time to compose it? Creating content that aligns with the SEO principles we discuss in other parts of this book helps, but some online battle outcomes are determined long before they happen.

Think about this: there are 10 million websites competing for a single keyword phrase that you are considering building content around. The top twenty currently ranked sites have been around for over 15 years, are highly optimized, have thousands of backlinks originating from sites with lots of authority, and a lot of social interaction tied to them. If you consider this scenario, the odds of displacing some of that content with something new might be slim or non-existent.

Let the Internet Boogeyman learn that lesson the hard way. You don't have to waste your time preparing content for battles you won't win.

What you DO need to know is the quality and quantity of the online competitors who are trying to get their content placed above yours for those same keywords on first page search engine results. In other words, how many other sites mention the targeted keywords you want to think about using, and how many of the most important SEO factors are already working in their favor?

Relevance and Intentions

The third thing you need to get a feel for is how RELE-VANT those words or phrases are to your offerings, as well as the intentions of the people using them in search engines. Is there commercial intent associated with the words or phrases people are typing into a search engine? Are they looking to invest money in a product, service or company that gives them what they're looking for? There is a big difference in commercial significance between a phrase like "how to get a, b, c and d" and a similar phrase like "how to get a, b, c and d at no charge."

Once you know which keywords people are typing into search engines (ones that are related to your business, that don't have too much or too strong of competition, that attract plenty of searches by people with an intention or willingness to spend money), then you have an advantage over any current or potential Internet Boogeymen. You know which words and phrases to embed in the content you create and distribute online. Most of them don't.

***Bonus: See http://www.BusinessWebVideos.com, register an account (FOR FREE) and you'll get access to our "secret weapons." If you want to know what our favorite KEYWORD RESEARCH tool/web application is and how you can use it to eliminate guesswork and spot important trends you otherwise might have missed, then this is your chance.

Here's a link to our favorite keyword research tool:

http://www.marketsamurai.com/c/buildatribe

(Yes, it is an affiliate link, and we will earn a few bucks if you buy it. Yes, we would recommend it even if we didn't. Yes, we use it, too.)

Chapter 3 - The Field of Battle and Rules of Engagement

How to Use Search Engines To Your Advantage

Basically the job of search engines is to locate and rank information on the web in priority order based on relevance. There are many factors which affect how search engines rank information.

If, in the eyes of the search engines, you do a better job than an Internet Boogeyman of creating and distributing content that promotes your name, company, products, services, knowledge and expertise in more (and better) places and ways, then you can win. In order for you to win, it is important to know what search engines like and what they don't. To CONTINUE winning, you need to know WHY so you can continually adapt and stay ahead of the Internet Boogeyman.

This is important for you to understand because, at some point, you might have to create YOUR content in ways that make it MORE appealing to the search engines than the work done by an Internet Boogeyman. If you are proactively trying to secure your places online, then you should do it right the first time and make it harder for an Internet Boogeyman to displace your work now or in the future.

The things we're writing about are not written in stone and can change at any time. It's more a compilation of data available in the public domain along with observations based on our personal test results and those of our online marketing friends.

We're not going to hesitate to offer opinions on hunches and trends that we see emerging either. Whether or not we can be helpful without being overly technical is our biggest challenge. Be patient with us.

Before we go further, we want to encourage you to let common sense be your guide. If something we suggest doesn't seem right to you, that's okay. Let your aggressiveness, style and motivation direct your actions ... whatever they may be.

As a word of advice: if you come up with ideas to "trick" the search engines, we encourage you to accept the probability that you are not the first, only or most technically skilled person to think of them and/or try to implement them. We aren't encouraging this method.

Before moving forward, we want to give a shout out of appreciation and credit where it is deserved. Over the years, there have been more than a few folks who have done a great job of compiling and documenting the additions, subtractions and relative changes in importance tied to Google's ranking factors.

If you want a detailed history, go online and check out Vaughn Aubuchon's compilation. (Type in "Vaughn's Summaries Google Ranking Factors SEO Checklist" into Google.) Or for an up-to-date summary, type in "Google's 200 ranking factors", and you will get a list of the most current factors and their descriptions. Brian Dean at www.Backlinko.com did a great job with his list, and we want to send some credit and praise his way. If you want to dig in deeper, then check out www.MOZ.com, www.SearchEngineJournal.com or invest some time at www.WarriorForum.com.

Wearing a White Hat

There are two sets of online marketing techniques people want to know about. Some are known as "white hat" and the others are known as "black hat".

"White hat" techniques are those that are generally accepted as fair and legitimate best practices. They help the search engines do their job and accurately reflect the content and its value to users. "Black hat" techniques are the exact opposite. They are the techniques that marketers use to game the systems and trick search engines into ranking information in places where it doesn't really belong.

"Black hat" efforts eventually come back to bite those using them, even if they offer short-term gains. Search engines get wise and sooner or later they change algorithms and their programming. Many of the "black hat" sites get penalized or, worse, banned. We aren't fans of "black hat" techniques and only share what we believe to be fundamentally safe and sound strategies that will serve you well in the future.

We don't want to make the mistake of assuming what you do or don't know about optimizing content for rankings in search engines. Let's spend a bit of time familiarizing you or refreshing your memory with some of the most popular terms, definitions and criteria being used by search engines to affect rankings.

Whenever you hear someone talk about SEO, they're referring to search engine optimization. It's nothing more than the study of how to increase the quantity and quality of the visits to a website by increasing a site's rank in search engine listings for specific words or phrases.

When people talk about a SERP, they are talking about the search engine results page which is just a listing of the results returned after a search has been performed.

Links

Let's talk about links, which are characters (usually text and sometimes images) on a webpage. They cause an Internet browser to send an Internet user to some other webpage or different place on the same webpage when a user clicks on them. Links are usually created because a person putting content on a website feels it adds value to others who might visit that page.

For example, a link might send someone to a place where they can get additional or supplemental information related to the topic they were investigating. A link might be a shortcut that makes it easier for someone to take action, buy something or register for something like a gift or additional information.

There are different types of links too. An outbound link is a link from your site to a different one. When you link to another site, it makes the other site look more valuable to search engines.

When two different sites link back and forth to each other, those links are referred to as a reciprocal link. The value of reciprocal links may suffer in comparison to non-reciprocal links because the possibility exists for collusion in the eyes of the search engines.

If everyone knew that links to their sites helped their rankings in search engines, then they could just go out and make deals with all types of different site owners. Then they could give each other links regardless of if those other sites contained relevant information. Over the years, people have already done this. The search engines adjusted accordingly so those trying to trick the system would not benefit.

By comparison, non-reciprocal are just the opposite. When Site X links to Site Y but the reverse isn't true, then those links are considered non-reciprocal links. Search engines place a little more value on these because the likelihood of collusion or a quid pro quo between sites is less likely.

Inbound links, or backlinks as they are often called, are the links from other peoples' sites to yours. These links are the MOST VALUABLE because they help tell search engines how much authority and trust to place on the site's information.

Think of backlinks like Internet endorsements. When there are lots of links to your site, the search engines register that it must be pretty important if so many people take the extra time necessary to place an outbound, non-reciprocal link on their site directed at yours.

It's not just the amount of links coming to your site that matter. Contextual links, which are links tied to words and sentences (or a paragraph of text instead of just stand alone links by footer or sidebar), are likely be more valuable.

If all of your site's backlinks are coming from one place, like the comments section in a forum, then they won't look as natural as links coming from a wide variety of other similarly themed sites.

If the links coming to your site originate from robust and thorough pieces of content - like a 2,000 word article or other original work that is enhanced by multimedia (containing things Podcasts and embedded YouTube videos) - you should get more love from search engines compared to a link from a negative remark or a badly written piece that is very similar, if not the same, as other online content.

A site's authority and credibility that links to yours is also relevant. Think about this. If CNN, FOX News, ESPN and several major U.S. newspapers placed links from their site to yours, that means a lot more search engines than 50 random links coming from small-town Mayberry residents.

The most valuable endorsements are sites that have existed for a long time and have lots of information, views and links directed toward them.

There are three main ways another website could link to yours:

1. Anchor Text – In this method, a keyword is used to create the linkable text on the page. For instance, if you have a website about home repair, then a link from another site with the words 'ceiling fan replacement' would be an anchor text link.

2. Branded – These types of links often have your business name or related moniker as the actual link. Bloggers and other website owners may share something about your company and link using the words 'ABC Home Repair'.

3. Generic – Probably the most common, these links are the ones you see the most. Words in these links are

phrases like 'click here' and 'learn more'. They don't really explain what the person clicking on the link is going to see when they get there, but that's ok.

In order to avoid an Internet Boogeyman, we recommend that your website have a *natural looking link profile* of all three types of links. Having too many of one type will hurt your overall rankings.

It's safe to say that there are hundreds of SEO factors that search engines use to rank results. Everything counts. As more competition pops up in your online marketing space, it becomes more important that your online content is aligned with as many of the following guidelines and best practices as possible.

Here is a word of caution: don't get so wrapped up with SEO techniques that the quality of your message suffers. Don't take content that's funny, interesting or authentic and turn it into boring, safe corporate speak that's easily forgettable just so you can include a bunch of SEO techniques. If you can create great content and present it in an authentic way that makes online consumers like/share/comment/discuss/forward it to others, then you will earn additional traffic and backlinks the natural way and the search engines will reward you.

When search engines want something, it is a really good idea to give it to them. If I wanted to, it wouldn't be hard to make a case that providing great content may be the best SEO tactic of all.

Time to Long Click

Imagine that two local companies had similar widgets to sell.

Let's suppose one thousand people type "Widget X" into the Google search engine while using the Chrome browser, which is owned by Google. Then they click a link to visit Company A's site for an average of five seconds and leave without doing anything else.

Then let's suppose that another thousand people enter "Widget X" in the search engine and click a link to visit Company B's site for an average of 17 minutes, share links to that site, and add lots of comments to the content. After that, the site visitors share the content they found on the site through all their social media channels.

What would that tell you if you analyzed all that data from the Chrome browser and the Google search engine? You would know the search terms Internet users typed into the search bar. You would know which pages they were clicking on. You would know how long visitors stayed on the various sites. You would know if they shared a comment or link to what they saw too.

In our example, you would come to an obvious conclusion: Company B's link was much more relevant, interesting and helpful to users typing "Widget X" into a search engine than Company A's. That's why you have to create content for humans AND for search engines. If you do a poor job of creating content for humans, it will be obvious and they won't like, refer or look at it for any length of time.

By looking at your website for an extended amount of time, something called a 'long click' is registered with Google. Since Google's ultimate goal is to provide the information their users are searching for, a long click is a signal to them that the user was happy with the result they were provided. Just as you analyzed that Company B's site had better information, so does Google – and they'll reward that site.

The amount or absence of social interaction surrounding your content sends valuable messages to search engines. Just like links send messages to search engines, think about what that number of tweets, Facebook likes and shares, Pinterest pins and more means to them too.

Websites develop authority over time based on popularity, quality content, traffic, links and shares. It only makes sense that similar inferences can be derived and, to a greater degree WILL be derived, from how Internet users interact with or don't interact with social media sites.

Having a business and a brand with a Facebook page, Twitter account, LinkedIn company page and Pinterest account with plenty of followers and likes sends a message of legitimacy to real people. They notice, so it makes sense that search engines would notice too.

SEO efforts can easily backfire if you go overboard with SEO techniques, if your work looks spammy, or if it looks like you're trying too hard to push certain words or phrases in robotic, unnatural ways. Since social media posts and pages can rank in search engines just like websites do, it's just as important to keep the same advice in mind when creating content for them.

The amount of weight search engines give to the following factors are somewhat of a moving target. It's the nature of the beast. Tough luck if you want strict rules and exacting measures. That's not how it works. All you can do is the best you can and remain flexible.

The good news is that you can do a lot more than others and do way more once you apply what we've got to share with you. If you want more "nitty-gritty" details, then read the Google Webmaster guidelines and spend time in the forums and sites we mentioned earlier.

There are on-page SEO factors and off-page SEO factors that affect your search engine rankings. With any of the on-page or off-page factors, some affect rankings DIRECTLY (because the search engines consider them in their algorithms). Other factors affect rankings INDIRECTLY (because they get people to generate links, stay on sites longer, interact with content, like, comment and share the content with others).

Positive On-Page Factors

On-page factors include the things you can do to your site's content that affect search engine rankings. Off-page factors are external to your site but still affect your search engine rankings.

Let's start by discussing some of the on-page SEO factors rumored to positively affect your site's search engine rankings.

Having your main keyword phrase in the domain name is crucial. Another related tip: when reading your domain name from left to right, the most important words should come first and second most important words should come next and so on. For example: www.mainkeywordphraseUSA.com would be preferable to www.USAmainkeywordphrase.com in the eyes of the search engines.

It is also correct to include hyphens between keywords. For example, www.mainkeywordphrase.com is good and www.Main-Keyword-Word-Phrase.com is appropriate too. We prefer the previous over the latter, but both can help. If you have four hyphens or more, it is probably going to look spammy, so we advise against it.

If you aren't a web designer and don't know what meta-tags are, it's all right. Your webmaster will. Some of you may be using template systems for building websites, and many of them will have boxes of fields marked appropriately where you can enter tags or descriptions. In any case, the following guidance should serve you well.

Remember to include your keywords in the title tag as close to the beginning as possible. Limit yourself to approximately 50 or 60 characters. It's also a good idea to avoid using special characters.

Your description meta-tag should be less than 150 or 160 characters and definitely contain the most important keywords and phrases. It's what shows up on the search engine results pages. It should be written in a way that interests and compels a user to click and learn more. Think of it as a 150 to 160 character "ad-copy" invitation designed to capture the attention and interest of your intended audience. Avoid using quotation marks or anything else except alphanumeric characters. Otherwise you run the risk of having search engines truncate your description or using something else altogether.

The search engines stopped using the meta keyword tag many years ago, so we advise against using it at all. In fact, we actually recommend against putting it on your website, since it's extra (and useless) code that the page has to load. Since the search engines take into account the speed at which your page loads, this is better left out altogether.

Learn more about which tags are important for your site with the free video at http://redcanoemedia.com/three-important-seo-tags/

Let's discuss the body of your text and some positive SEO factors.

Put your keywords and phrases in your page's section heading tags. Bigger, bolder and italicized keywords and phrases show emphasis to real people. Search engines will likely take notice too.

Try to put keyword phrases in exact matching order, which means using the same words in the same order. It can help you better connect with people who are typing that exact phrase in the search engines than it would if you just had those keywords spread out all over your page.

Place your keyword phrases earlier in your online text closer to the top of your page instead of near the bottom.

Use relevant keywords in the "alt text" when you get the chance to describe your images or graphics. If you don't know what "alt text" is, your webmaster will. Just tell your webmaster what relevant keywords or phrases you want to use to describe your graphics, as well as what images they go with.

While there used to be a need for keyword density tools, the recent Hummingbird update from Google virtually removed the need for such things. Instead of trying to put your keyword a certain number of times on your page, we recommend writing copy that sounds natural and uses words in the same way you'd use in a conversation.

For instance, if you're writing a page about pasta, the search engines expect to see words like *fork* and *sauce* and *meatball*. The search engines understand the relationship of these words and judge your page with those sort of things in mind.

Search engines and users pay attention to how often you update your site with new content. They also pay attention to the ratio of your site's old pages compared to new ones, so the more often you update and provide new content, the better.

Domain age and the number of years a domain has been registered are ranking factors. Registering a site for five or 10 years sends a message of stability and credibility to search engines.

Good spelling, grammar and outbound links to related sites send a message of congruence and quality to search engines. You might be rewarded because of it.

Having videos on your site (particularly YouTube videos since Google owns YouTube) sends a positive signal.

Bullet points and lists are appreciated by human viewers because they make things easier to read. Search engines also are rumored to more favorably view sites that present their information this way.

Think about it. Search engines, just like humans, like to see contact information, privacy policies and terms of service. Search engines know that spammers like to hide. So site owners who are easy to reach, take active steps to protect privacy, and describe the terms of their service are not as likely to be spammers. That's why search engines are more apt to view and rank their sites as more valuable.

Sites optimized for mobile devices are appreciated, and the word is out that it is a valuable and increasing quality factor.

On-Page Mistakes

What are some of the supposedly on-page SEO screw ups that might negatively affect your rankings?

Keyword stuffing, (i.e. overuse of keywords in the body, meta-tags and "alt text" that goes with your images) can harm your rankings. Notice that we said OVERUSE, not use. There is a difference.

The opposite may also cause problems. If you have too many keywords that are unrelated and not part of a congruent theme, your rankings could suffer from what is referred to as keyword dilution.

Just like you could be rewarded by people liking and sharing your original content, beware of using too many rude and offensive words.

It's also a bad idea to use content that belongs to someone else without giving them the credit, shout outs, links or attribution they deserve. Users can and do report copyright violations.

One trick that has been around since the beginning of time: putting a bunch of keywords in text format on a page using a text color that matches the background (with the intention of making the text look invisible). We know some people who tried and got away with this, and we assure others have tried it and been penalized.

This method goes against the spirit of normal user interaction. It's not a good idea to fraudulently affect rankings with trickery. As a matter of principle, we aren't fans and believe it will come back to bite those who do it sooner rather than later.

People don't like if your site has a bunch of pop-up advertisements and/or ads above the fold (i.e. the top half of your webpage) with relatively little content. It is a mistake to assume that the search engines would think differently.

Matt Cutts, the leader of the web spam team at Google, has indicated that there are other issues which are viewed as red flags by the search engines alone or when identified together with other factors. For example, if the site owner has been deemed by Google as a spammer, then the other sites owned by that person may be subjected to additional scrutiny. Sites where the "who is" information is marked as private make search engines question whether the owners are trying to hide something.

Additionally, if the site owner changes regularly, it can send messages to search engines worth taking note of. We advise against having identical or almost identical content with very few changes or modifications on the same site.

If you don't check that your link still works, you might be sending a message to search engines that your site has been neglected. Abandoned sites are not viewed as quality sites, and their rankings are likely to suffer.

Positive Off-Page Factors

Let's talk about some of the most popular off-page factors that can improve your rankings. Obviously we have touched on this before, but the quality of links coming to your site from other sites helps. The more trustworthy and heavily visited the sites that are providing links to your site, the better.

Other benefits: links directed toward your site with anchor text comprised of your keyword phrases help when the sites linking to yours offer related themes and content.

Be careful with this, though, as you don't want to have too many of these keyword-anchored links. The search engines will actually penalize you if they think your "link profile" is unnatural.

It's beneficial when visitors bookmark, spend time on or click on your pages and then go to and come from places that are related to your offerings. Why? Because it helps search engines get a clearer picture of how well your site is satisfying those who are typing specific related keywords in the search engines. The more satisfied your visitors appear, the greater the likelihood that search engines will keep referring visitors to your content.

Off-Page Mistakes

What are some of the off-page SEO screw ups that search engines don't like that can mess up your rankings? Well, just think about the opposite of the positive factors.

• Buying links instead of earning them is one way to negatively affect your work.

• Getting links from unrelated sites with unrelated themes and content can backfire too. Search engines are likely to reach conclusions regarding why links to your site exist if content seems unrelated. Purchased links, collusion and attempts to game the system all look bad.

• Having few, if any, links from external sites directed toward yours can also be a problem.

• Utilizing unreliable servers that are frequently down is a big negative.

This is not an exhaustive list, but at least you have an idea about what matters most and, more importantly, the spirit of WHY things matter. Trust your instincts to avoid online choices that steer you to do something tricky or un-natural.

In our opinion, one of the biggest obstacles people must overcome is what to type into the search engines in the first place. At some point (maybe not that far in the future) don't be surprised if the search engines do a better job of giving users what they want, even if it isn't what they typed into the search engine.

Recognize the power of browsers and search engines to track what you type in, where you go, how long you stay, what you like and what you don't like based on your behaviors while you're online. Tricking search engines is not a long-term strategy for success.

By comparison, what is? Think like your ideal client.

Give them the content they want, the way they want it, in the places where they like to spend their time online, and on the devices they like to use (computers, tablets, phones, televisions, etc.) Describe what that content contains, who it's for and align with the systems the search engines and social media sites have created for analyzing and ranking that content. You'll be better off because of it.

Chapter 4 - Strategic and Tactical Fundamentals

Purchasing URLS/Domain Names

It's no secret that having a keyword in the URL/domain is a heavily weighted SEO factor when it comes to search engine rankings. Take control of key URLs/domains before the Internet Boogeyman does.

Your Name:

If you want to protect your name, then buy domain names like YourName.com. As a second line of defense, consider adding YourNameReviews.com and YourNameReview.com if you sell expertise, knowledge or consulting services branded with your name.

If you want to pre-empt potential damage caused by "hater sites", then consider picking up YourNameSucks.com, YourNameRipoffs.com, YourNameRipoff.com, YourNameScams.com or YourNameScam.com. Domain names are inexpensive, so it might be a wise move, however you can also go crazy trying to acquire all of the related phrase domains. Don't drive yourself mad.

Even if you don't have an Internet Boogeyman bothering you now, acquiring URLs/domain names like those suggested above can build authority (domain age) starting now instead of later (when you might need it).

You can always increase the number of years your URL/domain is registered for in the future. You also can create sites and add relevant (and keyword loaded) content, as well as links to relevant directories and social media accounts. (We will go into more detail on this later in the book.)

The point is that YOU want to own those URLs/domain names, not the Internet Boogeyman. You need the domain age working in your favor, and you want to control the number of years the domain is registered for.

Important note: Once you've purchased these domain names, we do not recommend that you forward all of them to your main site. While in the past this was a common practice, we have actually heard stories of an Internet Boogeyman building poor links to a company's forwarded domain, thus causing his main site to be penalized. This practice is virtually untraceable because the links weren't directly pointed to his main site. Instead, buy these domains and use a feature called 'parking' to hold onto them so no one else can get them.

Your Company/Product/Service Names:

To protect your company name, product name or services name, then the same advice as previously stated applies for the same reasons.

To protect your company name, consider the following:

YourCompanyName.com

YourCompanyNameReviews.com/
YourCompanyNameReview.com

YourCompanyNameScams.com/
YourCompanyNameScam.com

YourCompanyNameRipOffs.com/
YourCompanyNameRipOff.com

To protect a product name, consider the following:

YourProductName.com

YourProductNameReviews.com/
YourProductNameReview.com

YourProductNameScams.com/
YourProductNameScam.com

YourProductNameRipOffs.com/
YourProductNameRipOff.com

To protect a service name, you might want to consider:

YourServiceName.com

YourServiceNameReviews.com,
YourServiceNameReview.com

YourServiceNameScams.com,
YourServiceNameScam.com

YourServiceNameRipOffs.com,
YourServiceNameRipOff.com

If you have one or two profitable keyword phrases that drive significant revenue to your business, then protect them too.

For example, if you get many leads from people who find your business when looking for a tanning salon in Anytown USA, then secure URLs/domains like TanningSalonAnytown.com and AnytownTanningSalon.com. If you want to be REALLY thorough, pick up the plural versions of those URLs/domains TanningSalonsAnytown.com and AnytownTanningSalons.com.

Acquiring Social Media Accounts

Important social media accounts carry a lot of weight in search engines. Social media account sites can (and should) be optimized just like websites. When social media accounts are created, most give you the opportunity to enter keyword loaded descriptions, titles and tags. Just another reason why the keyword research discussed earlier is SO important!

We think it is a good idea to first create and then optimize your main social media accounts. Optimize your accounts much like you would your website, and BE SURE to use your keywords. Link your social media accounts together whenever possible, and add relevant and keyword optimized content on a REGULAR basis.

At the very least, set up optimized and keyword loaded accounts for your business. Create another set of accounts for yourself as an individual person too.

Adding fresh, quality content on a regular basis sounds like a lot of work. It can, but it doesn't have to be. We'll explain (and give you access to a secret weapon that automates the process!)

The Manual Process:

If you are going to set up/manage/share your information manually, then it is a good idea to first invest work in the biggest and most powerful social networks. If you're only going to have time to manage a few, we encourage you to start with Facebook, Twitter, YouTube, Google Plus, LinkedIn, Pinterest and Instagram.

We still recommend that you also secure your business and personal names for emerging social media accounts. First of all, we want you to get your hands on the emerging social media accounts before an Internet Boogeyman does. Second of all, we want you to get your hands on emerging social media accounts BEFORE they become the next big thing (like a Facebook or YouTube). Finally, links to and from these social media accounts add relevance and authority to your existing web presence, making it even tougher for an Internet Boogeyman to displace your work.

Using Service Providers:

Do you have to do all the work creating accounts for yourself? The answer is no.

If you're tempted to save a few dollars and hire an outsourced offshore worker using a site like ODesk.com, there are risks you should be aware of. What would you do if the worker you hired became an Internet Boogeyman or shares information with someone who becomes one? Can you prove your usernames and passwords when he lives halfway around the world and you've never met? Even if you could prove it, will it be too late because the damage is already done? Do you have any real recourse when he isn't subject to our laws?

We are big fans of Knowem.com where you can currently purchase 25 to 300 social media accounts optimized and created for approximately $85 to $650. They've already identified more than several thousand different social media services even though only a few hundred are shown on their site. For a nominal monthly fee, they will register your organization with 20 to 30 new sites that come out each month.

In our initial conversation with Michael Streko, the co-founder of Knowem.com, he went to great lengths to describe the rigorous pre-employment background check and screening process. They use American workers who are held in check with strict confidentiality and non-disclosure agreements, as well as background checks to protect their customers.

Whether you want to create the accounts yourself or not, Knowem.com also allows you to personally check the availability of usernames for hundreds of social media accounts free of charge. In a matter of minutes, you can discover how vulnerable you really are. Hopefully you find out by visiting Knowem.com before a wannabe Internet Boogeyman does.

Getting Your Website Listed With Local Directories

Directory registrations are a good move if you want to lock up more listings on the first page of search results for your name and business name (and maybe even a few keyword phrases tied to your industry and local area). Because listings in well-established directories typically rank high in search engines, it can be difficult for an Internet Boogeyman to displace them. Plus many give you the opportunity to add backlinks (from trusted sites with high authority) to your main website, and they are never penalized as long as the content is relevant.

Website directories are sites that list websites by categories. For example, there are directories that list businesses by geographical areas or industries. A good example would be a site like www.Manta.com. There also are directories of more websites listed by category at sites like www.a1webdirectory.org.

Getting registered in RESPECTED directories is another off-page action that can affect your search engine rankings a positive way. In many cases, it costs little or nothing to register your site with many popular website directories.

The first thing you need to do is find a directory. To get you started, we will give you a list of some popular ones. Then create an account and fill in the business information it requests.

The needed information is typically your name, business name, phone number, address, hours of operation, a product or service description (a great opportunity to load keywords!) and a LINK to your website! If a directory lets you add pictures and/or videos, have them ready to upload. Make sure you take the time to add as many relevant categories as a directory will allow. And don't forget to enter the submit or register button.

One final step is to check your email shortly after registering. It's important since most directories will send an email confirmation link you will need to click on to verify your listing.

Another tip is to make sure that all the information you submit to one directory is the same as what you do for others. This mainly refers to the basic information like your name, company name, address and phone number (NAP). Don't put 405 E. 5th St. in one directory, 405 East 5th Street in another, and 405 E. Fifth St. in another. Be consistent.

The bad news is that it can be time consuming to create listings in lots of directories. The good news is that many, if not most of them, have FREE basic listings that are more than adequate for your needs. And once you create and verify your listing, there's not much else you need to do.

Some directories do charge upgrade fees. Registering your website in Yahoo's directory can cost a few hundred dollars per year, but it sends a message to search engines about your non-spammy legitimacy.

As of the date of this writing, here are some great places to start:

http://www.supermedia.com

http://www.yellowpages.com

http://www.merchantcircle.com

https://www.google.com/business/placesforbusiness/

https://www.bingplaces.com/

http://www.local.com

http://www.hotfrog.com

http://www.manta.com

http://www.yelp.com

http://www.infousa.com

http://www.ibegin.com

http://www.localpages.com

http://www.yellowbot.com

http://www.yellowusa.com

http://www.ezlocal.com

Getting Your Blog(s) Listed in Blog Directories

It makes sense to register your blog site(s) with blog directories for the same reasons it is logical to get a business website listed in local directories. When you get backlinks to your blog (and additional traffic) from highly trusted and authoritative sites, then you are better prepared to displace and/or suppress the efforts of an Internet Boogeyman on search engine's first pages.

There are numerous worthwhile blog directories. Some are manually edited, and others want to see ESTABLISHED blogs that have been in existence before they get listed (i.e. approximately 12 posts over the course of at least six months).

The point is to start NOW if you haven't already. An Internet Boogeyman who creates a "hater" blog site to smear you might have to wait (and/or have time to cool off) before he can do the same.

These can change but, as of the date of this publication, here are a few blog directories that we think are worthwhile:

http://www.bloggeries.com/

http://www.spillbean.com/

http://www.bloggingfusion.com/

http://www.bloghints.com/

http://www.blogflux.com/

http://globeofblogs.com/

Creating Content and Building Your Online Presence - Automation/Syndication

One of the main reasons we like bowling (as a matter of principle) is the same as the reason we like distributing content on the Internet. In bowling, you can roll a ball and knock down a single pin or a bunch of them with the same effort. The process for creating and distributing content on the Internet works almost the same way.

Every syndicated writer, radio or television show host who has ever been successful will tell you that one of their main goals was to get syndicated. Why? Because they were passionate and knowledgeable about their topics and wanted to make a difference in as many peoples' lives as possible. They also wanted exponential increases in their salaries without the proportional increase in their workloads.

When a columnist writes one article and it gets published in one newspaper, he reaches one audience and gets one check. When many newspapers want to publish that same article, it can reach additional audiences and the columnist gets additional checks. Syndication means that his audience increases, his paycheck increases but his workload doesn't.

Writers, television and radio show hosts can broadcast syndicated content worldwide and reach an almost limitless number of people thanks to automation and technology. So can you.

We use a secret weapon that AUTOMATICALLY distributes original content along with the title, tags, and keyword loaded descriptions that search engines value to lots of different places in various forms as if you did it manually. After we tell you what it does and how it works, we're going to tell you what it is and how to get it too. When used regularly, it will make it almost impossible for an Internet Boogeyman, or even a team of them working together, to manually keep pace with your automated content production and distribution systems.

Want to discourage Internet Boogeymen? Want them scratching their heads wondering how you can stay so far ahead of them and in so many different places? If so, you're going to love this.

For the sake of discussion, let's assume you produced a piece of content that answered a question you or your business gets regularly from potential clients. Your next objective is to distribute it to all of the online social media and websites that matter most. In other words, you want your content piece in video format version so it can go not only to YouTube, but also to other highly viewed video sites. You also want it in podcast format (and then distributed to the most popular podcast sites so it can be available for download). Other highlights: strip the video script into text (so it can go to blog sites and article posting sites) and post updates on your status sites like Facebook, Twitter and others (so you can let your friends, fans and followers know about where they can access your new content).

If you create a video, there are more than a few sites that we believe are worth distributing it to. It's overwhelming to upload your video one at a time to 10 different places and enter the keyword loaded data that describes your video to search engines 10 different times.

And that's just to get a single video to all the sites. When you include the time it takes to get your content to blog /article/status/podcast sites, you can definitely see it's an enormous undertaking.

The secret weapon we're about to share will give you an unfair advantage when competing with your rivals. If you use automation and they operate manually, then YOU should rest easier at night.

What if you could just upload your content once along with the accompanying keyword loaded descriptive text and press a button that would upload and distribute your content to lots of places for you? Imagine being able to upload a video/article/podcast once and press a single button to have your content sent to all kinds of important places as if you did it yourself?

As we published in our book *Attract, Capture & Convert* (see http://www.AttractCaptureConvertBook.com), here are some great places to distribute your content in various formats. You may do it manually or use the link below to find out how we AUTOMATE the distribution of content to most of the best sites that are listed.

Video Sites:

http://youtube.com

http://dailymotion.com

http://videobash.com

http://dekhona.com

http://iviewtube.com

http://metacafe.com

http://photobucket.com

http://tagworld.com

http://veoh.com

http://vidipedia.org

Podcast Sites:

http://everypodcast.com

http://podcast.com

http://podcastblaster.com

http://plazoo.com

Blog Sites:

http://blogger.com

http://tumblr.com

http://livejournal.com

http://squidoo.com

http://wordpress.com

Social Bookmarking Sites:

http://reddit.com

http://slashdot.org

http://bibsonomy.org

http://folkd.com

http://memotoo.com

http://saveyourlinks.com

http://startaid.com

http://stumbleupon.com

http://whitelinks.com

Status Sites:

http://linkedin.com

http://pinterest.com

http://facebook.com

http://twitter.com

http://plurk.com

http://sokule.com

http://friendfeed.com

Article Sites:

http://articlecity.com

http://articletrader.com

http://articlecube.com

http://articlesnatch.com

http://earticlesonline.com

http://homebiztools.com

http://blogwidow.com

http://premierdirectory.org

http://searcharticles.net

http://triond.com

http://workoninternet.com

http://look-4it.com

Doing it manually takes a long time. This is a MUCH better way.

Here's our affiliate link. They pay us a referral fee (without raising the cost to you), but we would recommend this service even if they didn't.

www1.instantcustomer.com/cmd.php?af=75353

If the link doesn't work or changes after this book is published, feel free to visit http://www.BusinessWebVideos.com and register a free account that will also give you updated access to this link, as well as our other most popular secret weapons.

Chapter 5 - The Secret Weapon

The Most Powerful Weapon Online
(*other than great keyword research*)

What is the most powerful weapon in your arsenal when it comes to doing battle with an Internet Boogeyman? Without a doubt, we think it is video.

There are several reasons why. They grab attention in search engines. They can outrank websites in search engines. They wield excessive and disproportionate influence.

Grabbing Attention in Search Engine Listings

The next time you view a search engine result page that contains a video link, notice how the picture of the video makes it capture your attention. It's hard not to notice the video because it stands out.

If the Internet Boogeyman's goal is to embarrass, humiliate and damage you and your business, then don't be surprised if he creates videos to tell his story because he already know what we are telling you. Videos stand out, visually speaking, in search engine results when compared with the rest of the listings that are simply made of text.

Outranking Websites in Search Engines

Do some videos outrank websites? How does that happen?

YouTube is owned by Google. YouTube makes money when companies buy advertising on videos that get played. Google wants YouTube to make lots of money, and it has a vested interest in helping videos get more views. Google gives preferential treatment to YouTube videos.

If you want to maximize the ability of any videos you create to rank in search engines. then there is a SPECIFIC formula you MUST follow. If you do and your Internet Boogeyman doesn't (because he isn't likely to know what we are getting ready to tell you), then you have another HUGE advantage.

Because videos take extra time to create (when compared to spammy text), the quality factor associated with this style of content is highly regarded by Google and other search engines. We believe higher quality videos (i.e. high definition) are viewed as an additional quality factor and receive even more preferential treatment in search engines.

If you would like your videos to be found on search engines, it is imperative to use your keyword and keyword phrases. If your video does not meet ALL of the following criteria, its ability to rank in search engines will be SIGNIF-ICANTLY limited.

1. Your target keyword phrase or phrases should be in the title of your video.

2. Your target keyword phrase or Phrases should be in the description of your video.

3. Include your target keyword phrase or phrases in the script/content of the video, and make sure you speak clearly. *

4. Include your target keyword phrase or phrases in the TAGS when you upload your video.

*We believe this is a critical step because Google transcribes audio into text (for closed captioning purposes) and indexes the content as if it were indexing that same text. If you mumble or background noise prevents YouTube from accurately identifying your keywords, then you lose an advantage you should have had.

Audio clarity is also one of the two main reasons why it is often worth the investment to create videos in a controlled/studio environment. Shooting in high definition is the second because these HD videos also appear to get special treatment.

CAUTION! If you don't know the best keywords, your online marketing and targeted traffic will suffer. In case you missed it earlier, here's a link to our favorite keyword research tool:

http://www.marketsamurai.com/c/buildatribe

(It is an affiliate link, and we will earn a few bucks if you buy it. We use it and would recommend anyway.)

If you have an Internet Boogeyman who is harming your business or reputation using YouTube videos, then the chances are pretty good that he doesn't know what we just told you. If you do it right (by following the guidelines we just shared) and he doesn't, then there is a really good chance that your video will bump his from the "prime slots" on the search engine result pages.

Excessive and Disproportionate Influence:

Do you remember writing book reports in school? Do you remember reading assignments in college?

We do. As soon as we got a book report assignment in middle school, we would ask our teachers questions about the minimum number of pages required and whether or not pages with pictures counted. In college, the syllabus indicated how many pages of reading were assigned and REQUIRED before the next class.

Reading was assigned. It was homework. Our grades depended on it and, if we wanted good grades, we HAD to read even if we would rather have been doing something else. It's for those reasons people often associate reading with work.

Let's talk about television and movies by comparison. As a culture, we view those forms of media as "fun" and "entertainment". Kids beg their parents to watch more television. People love going to the movies. When was the last time you heard students complaining about HAVING to watch too much television or HAVING to go to the movies?

Additionally, consider this. Do you have a favorite actor/actress, sports hero or musician that you would LOVE to invite over to your house and hang out for a day? Imagine how cool it would be to chill with your favorite celebrities! Where would you go? What would you talk about? What would you do? Wouldn't it be awesome?

How do you know? You don't REALLY know them, do you? In real life, they could be TOTALLY different than what you expect. They could be TOTAL jerks!

It FEELS like you do know them though, doesn't it? Why? It's because you've seen them on television, video interviews or in the movies. You feel like you are connecting with them because video makes it feel like you are there with them.

I'm a fan of Ted Talks. For those of you who don't know what they are, they consist of 18 minute speeches from various experts and interesting individuals with unique perspectives and ideas worth sharing.

Recently I went to see an event in St. Louis that was hosted at the Missouri History Museum. On this particular day, I joined about 150 people to watch a live streaming video simulcast of the live Ted Talk event being hosted in Canada.

When the first speaker was finished, the crowd erupted with applause. They were so captivated by the video of the first person speaking that they "forgot" they were clapping to a video screen instead of a live person.

I've never seen a group of people clap at the end of a book. I have seen them clap at the end of a movie. That day I watched them clap at a movie screen of a speaker who wasn't even there.

The power of video to connect people and ideas on an emotional level is unmatched by text. Do not leave this power unchecked in the hands of an Internet Boogeyman! Do not forfeit your strength to use this exceptionally effective weapon in your arsenal.

Content Ideas

Do you need ideas for creating content? Maybe we can help.

Around here, we're big fans of the work done by an Internet marketer in San Diego named Mike Koenigs. As a starting point, Mike encourages businesses to produce videos that answer the 10 most FREQUENTLY ASKED questions, as well as the 10 most important SHOULD ASK questions. The "Should Ask" questions are the ones that customers probably WOULD ask if they knew as much about your products, services or industry as you did. Videos that provide this kind of exceptional content are the ones that EARN links, likes and social media shares that affect search engine ranking of your content.

Our friend Tom Ruwitch is the president of an email marketing firm here in St. Louis called Market Volt (see http://www.MarketVolt.com). He encourages business owners to create videos that answer buyer objections.

People love stories. If you don't provide them, your Internet Boogeymen might if they aren't already. Any stories you can tell that build value for what you do, what you know and who you are while teaching, entertaining or motivating your ideal clients can be a great thing. Transformation stories and testimonials enhance your credibility.

Misperceptions or false rumors that could or are being spread by an Internet Boogeyman can be addressed in your original works of content. This may be a viable option for telling your side of a story that needs to be told.

Reviews, comparisons and buyer advice provide you with starting points for future content creation. Don't be shy about mentioning potential mistakes and consequences tied to them.

It's often okay for you to talk about your mistakes and the lessons you learned for several reasons. First, it shows you're authentic and human. Second of all, your willingness to share your experiences so others don't suffer unnecessarily can make you and your company more endearing.

Special reports, shocking statistics, case studies and research can be the source of great content too. Be sure to cite the source. When you provide valuable ideas that protect the public from financial losses, embarrassment or unnecessary extra work, they recognize it and are much more likely to share your content, link to it and drive up your rankings in search engines.

Common Mistakes

There are a handful of common mistakes you can avoid. If you are going to invest the time and resources necessary to create video content, you might as well do it right the first time.

1.   Stuffing too many keywords at the beginning of a video can repel the audience you want to reach and come off as disingenuous. It's better to introduce yourself, state who the video content is created for, and show how it can help them (i.e. what are the benefits of watching it). Then give the viewers information they want.

2.   Whenever you title a video, be sure it is relevant and the content delivers on that promise. Don't suggest that viewers will get X and then give them Y.

3.   Less is usually more. You are better off creating 10 one-minute videos that answer one question or address

one topic each than you are to create one video that lasts 10 minutes and tries to cover it all at once. When battling with an Internet Boogeyman, lots of links/likes/shares/content pieces that take up tons of listings in search engine result pages are better than a few.

4. Don't date your content. In other words, try not to unnecessarily reference people, events or circumstances that could make your content seem out of date before it is necessary. For example, it adds no incremental value to your content if you did a video about a time management advantage of a particular product and referenced the recent Super Bowl Champion. But it will make your video seem old after a year or two even if the time management advantage of your product still remains.

5. Particularly with YouTube (as of the date of this writing), be sure to include the ENTIRE URL/domain name in your video's description. Include the http://www. with the URL/domain you would like to link to. Why? It will become an active backlink from a high authority site like YouTube.com. Many videos create backlinks directed at your other content, social media sites and websites from a high authority site like YouTube.com. You don't want to miss out on this advantage.

Done For You

Some people don't want to be on camera. There are plenty of reasons why they shouldn't, and that's okay.

Some people get (and REALLY) look nervous, and that might turn off viewers. Other people might not speak clearly (and Google can misinterpret their words, which could harm their search engine rankings). Some are SO critical of themselves that NOTHING done in front of a camera would look good enough for them.

Because most professional studios charge about $1,000 per finished minute of video, the price of HD video can be prohibitive to many business owners no matter how much an Internet Boogeyman is roughing them up. As an alternative, business owners might explore the idea of buying their own cameras, lighting, studio space and editing their own videos. Eventually many find out how time consuming it is to create their own but don't see any other alternative. For those reasons, we created http://www.BusinessWebVideos.com, where business owners can upload a script, pick a model and get it produced and distributed for 90 to 95% less than other high-end studios charge.

The videos at BusinessWebVideos utilize HD and professional models who know how to speak clearly. Since the main purpose is to get content ranked in search engines and connected with a specific audience, a streamlined and versatile video (without the distracting, "over-the-top" bells and whistles) fits the bill in most cases.

Chapter 6 - Offline Fundamentals

Hiring the Right People

Do your hiring decisions solve business problems or do they create new and different ones?

When it comes to employee screening and ultimately selecting your team members, hiring choices are only as solid as the information on which they are based. If your business doesn't take advantage of every opportunity that is legally available to gather relevant job-related background data on applicants BEFORE making job offers, it's like agreeing to play Russian Roulette without first checking all the chambers in the weapon.

We used to work with a sales rep from a pre-employment testing company named Syd Robinson. He said that resumes belonged in the library listed under fiction. Why? According to Syd, resumes were simply balance sheets with no liabilities.

Experienced human resource executives and experts we've spoken to over the years often suggest that about one-third of resumes are exaggerated. We've heard others say that as many as 70% of applications contain embellishments too. When you consider the fibs on applications and "creative writing" on resumes, it's hard to distinguish fact from fiction.

We think it's a good idea to perform background checks on potential applicants. Violent and reckless individuals on your payroll increase your risk of creating bad customer experiences and inspiring Internet Boogeymen.

For example, let's pretend that you want to hire a delivery driver and give him a delivery van with your company name on it. You fail to check into the applicant's background. Knowing about the applicant's history of careless and imprudent driving violations and road rage incidents would be a good idea before turning him loose while representing you and your company in the public's eye. With all the dash cams and mobile phones, the last thing you're going to want to see going viral is a YouTube video of your employee cutting people off, yelling obscenities or assaulting other drivers.

Will background checks protect you from hiring misfits and troublemakers who could act in ways that would fuel the fires of Internet Boogeymen? Yes and no. It's a good start, but it's not enough.

There are shortcomings too. It's important to recognize that a criminal background check only proves that an applicant was caught doing something wrong and successfully prosecuted. What about people who did things they shouldn't have done but didn't get caught? Or what about people who got caught but didn't get prosecuted or prosecuted successfully even though they were guilty?

If you haven't considered drug testing job applicants, maybe you should. Businesses who drug test will often tell you that it deters some drug addicts from even applying. And, even though employers have signs telling applicants that they will conduct drug tests, many STILL fail. If an applicant knows he will be tested and lacks the judgement and/or discipline to stay clean for 30 days so he can pass, then you may have averted the numerous potential disasters that could have occurred once that person got put on your payroll.

What about reference checks?

Many employers perform reference checks because occasionally a person who gets listed as a character reference or previous employer will reveal the ugly truth. For fear of getting sued, we understand why lots of former employers hesitate to verify more than previous employment dates, but the bottom line is that you can't get answers to important questions if you don't ask!

Using temporary employees or giving new hires a 30, 60, or 90 day probationary period is also a precautionary employee screening step worth considering. Surely some people can put on a show for a trial period, but not all of them.

Beyond those fundamental steps, which not everyone does, there is one more strategy worth mentioning. And it may be the most powerful and useful of all.

We are big fans of using properly validated pre-employment assessments. Some people are afraid to use them because they're worried about getting sued. The reality is that you can get sued for anything. Just ask McDonald's after they got stuck for making their coffee too hot.

It might actually be your best defense to use properly validated pre-employment tests and assessments that have been proven and documented as non-discriminatory by age, race and sex (not only against hiring mistakes, but also against discriminatory hiring practices). Assessments, along with the other selection methods mentioned, should only be used as PART of a fair and consistent selection process (not the single reason for a hire/no hire decision).

When combined with all the other selection methods mentioned earlier, assessments could actually be your best DEFENSE against discrimination charges or other unfair hiring practices. The reason this is true is because most of the best assessments are computer scored and computers don't care if people are black, white, male, female or martian.

We see tremendous value in the assessment and screening of basic skills in potential job applicants. If they don't possess basic math, vocabulary, spelling or problem solving skills, then you are inviting bad customer experiences, online reviews and ridicule that could have been prevented. In almost any job, those traits are necessities.

In addition to basic skills, we also see merit in assessments that identify things like integrity, reliability, work ethic and attitudes toward substance abuse. Why? Because we believe it is important that employers find people who have attitudes and values that match those required by the job. These types of pre- employment tests do a nice job of providing the missing pieces of an applicant's true picture and filling in whatever informational gaps remain after performing background checks, drug tests and reference checks.

We also see significant value in tests and assessments that reveal insights into behavioral traits like assertiveness, flexibility, organization, social need, competitiveness, sensitivity and tension. Why? We think there are SO many OBVIOUS mistakes that can be avoided if employers utilize this type of testing. For example, consider what would happen if a customer service role required someone to be empathetic, flexible and relaxed and the applicant you hired was really aggressive, insensitive and pushy?

One thing most employers don't think about (or even realize) is one of the most powerful features of the best pre-employment tests and assessments. What is it? The best tests and assessments have built in "distortion scores" or "lie scales" that indicate to potential employers when an applicant may be trying too hard to give answers they think the employer wants to hear. Individuals "fake good" all the time during interviews (and that's part of what makes them less reliable and unpredictable).

Unfortunately, there's no magical way to identify attempts to "fake good" during interviews with any degree of certainty beyond a "gut feel". Your interviewing system would be much better if you knew when applicants were lying and/or embellishing. It would make a HUGE difference, wouldn't it?

That's why a "lie scale" or "distortion score" on a properly developed assessment is SO valuable! It makes it MUCH easier for an interviewer to get the information he needs to show informed decisions and avoid unnecessary and expensive mistakes.

Whatever you decide your hiring process is, it must be consistent in order to be fair. For each position you try to fill, the first step to the last still needs to be the same for all applicants.

For example, let's say that I am thinking about hiring Billy or Suzie for an open position. Let's pretend that I've known Suzie's family for 15 years and Suzie since she was a little kid. If the last step in my selection process for this job is a background check and drug test and I decide to hire Suzie without putting her through those steps, then Billy has a legitimate beef if he were held to a more rigorous level of scrutiny. Whatever position you are trying to fill, make sure your steps are fair and consistent.

Anthony Robbins said, "Success leaves clues." We think he's right. When it comes to your top performers, how do you find those clues? Frank Sproule, an Atlanta-based organizational development consultant, once told us, "If you

don't know what made you a great team, how can you expect to continue the process?"

What can you do to determine what made you a great
team? How can you utilize your human resource information as a corporate asset and in ways that help you make
better employee selection, development and retention decisions faster?

Step 1. Take Inventory of Your Human Assets (Assess
Everyone)

Step 2. Identify Your Top Performers and Build Models That DEFINE Success For Each Position

Step 3. Hire, Develop and Manage in Ways That Minimize or Eliminate the Gaps

What if it were possible for you to create an inventory
management system for your talent just like many of you
have for the products in your warehouses? What would it
look like and how would it work?

*NOTE: SUPER BONUS. As of the date of this print-
ing, if you visit
http://www.ReverseRiskConsulting.com and invest approximately 3 to 5 minutes answering some basic ques-tions,
it is likely that you can get the following entirely FUNDED
for your company regardless of size. It's basi-cally an inventory management system for your talent. That's right. We
are talking about potentially tens of thousands of dollars in
savings delivered to you AT NO CHARGE and without
further obligation.

* Online behavioral assessment of ALL your employees (regularly $60 per person).

* A custom built website (your inventory management system for your talent).

* Training on how to utilize the data to evaluate the match between individuals and a job, as well as the match between individuals and a supervisor.

When it asks who referred you, be sure to mention this book title. If you think this sounds too good to be true, fill out the questionnaire and see for yourself.

Customer-Friendly Business Policies and Empowered/Trained Employees

Have you ever heard the saying, "Fight fire with fire?" When it comes to dealing with customers, try water instead. When you take care of a customer, you may solve an Internet Boogeyman problem before it ever occurs. If you go above and beyond what a customer expects to receive as far as service goes, then you might actually turn what could have been a vocal opponent into one of your biggest fans.

I live in St. Louis, Missouri, and I wanted a Porsche Boxster convertible. I visited the website Cars.com and created a search for all the Porsche Boxsters for sale within a 500-mile radius. For several months, I invested significant time checking out prices and CarFax reports on anything that came up meeting my criteria.

Then one day it showed up in my search results. A car that appeared to be exactly what I was looking for got listed. It had a metallic grey exterior. The interior was made of black leather. It only had 28,000 miles, but it was in Des Moines, Iowa at Stew Hansen Hyundai. It was a dealership with upfront pricing and what they were asking for this car was fair.

I called up the dealership and spoke with a sales rep named Bryan. I peppered him with all kinds of questions. He answered them perfectly, and I agreed to put down a deposit and make the trip to Des Moines to see this car for myself. My deposit was made on the contingency that this car was everything he described. I also insisted on a warranty so I wouldn't get stuck in the middle of nowhere Iowa (or Missouri for that matter) if it broke down on my way back.

To be safe, I went online and read the reviews of this automotive dealership. The comments about the dealership and my sales representative were positive. The CarFax reports looked good too.

The sales manager got involved and offered me a one-month, 1,000-mile warranty on the drive train and anything they inspected. I bought it.

When I got home with the car, it appeared there was a problem that wasn't on the drive train or their list of inspected items. It looked like I might have a problem that wouldn't be covered by our agreement.

I called the sales manager who could have insisted I drive the vehicle back to their location in Des Moines to examine and/or service it. He also could have told me that it wasn't his problem.

And, technically speaking, it wasn't his problem. It was mine.

And if he did, then you might be reading a very different story. I wouldn't have praised this dealership in my books, videos, articles, blogs or social media accounts. I was a frustrated customer, and he turned me into a fan and evangelist for their dealership! He didn't know I was a professional speaker or author. He just attempted to help me solve a problem.

He suggested that I visit the local Porsche dealership here in St. Louis and have them take a look. He asked me to call and let him know what the bill was. He offered to defray costs even though we both knew he didn't have to.

In the end, the "problem" was more of an "operator error" because I hadn't read my owners' manual yet. I appreciated the attentiveness and genuine effort made by that dealership to help me. I'm a fan!

Both my sales rep and the sales manager at Stew Hansen Hyundai understood what many others don't. Exceptional customer service at the brick and mortar OFFLINE level can be the best ONLINE sales and promotional strategy there is.

I didn't care what their ads said or how much they spent. I didn't care about their name recognition or their great selection of cars.

They did the "extras" that made me happy, and I want to tell others about it. I feel COMPELLED to tell others.

Word of mouth spreads fast. Words on keyboards do as well and they aren't often or easily erased. Make SURE your employees know the consequences (and rewards) tied to their words and interactions with customers.

I heard another story of a retail sporting goods store who sold a regulation size street hockey goal made out of plastic. The manufacturer made a clip that attached the net to the frame, but it had one major design flaw. It was only a matter of time until a street hockey puck would hit and break the clip.

The manufacturer knew this and even included an extra clip in their packaging. It wasn't enough. So the manufacturer distributed additional replacement clips to their customers through the retail store.

Eventually customers would get tired of driving back to the store and buying more clips. They kept complaining. They complained so much that the manufacturer eventually redesigned the clips.

One customer got so upset after multiple trips to the store for the same flawed part that he called the manufacturer. When he did, he found out that the re-engineered part existed. He was livid and went straight to the retail store to speak with the manager.

Unfortunately, this particular store had over 50,000 different items (SKUs) and, since the manufacturer didn't recall the old parts with the design flaw, the old parts got mixed in with the re-engineered parts on the retail floor. The manager had no idea.

What did the manager do when confronted by a justifiably angry customer? He didn't make excuses. He apologized, empathized and took action congruent with his words. He refunded the price of the entire goal as compensation for the customer's frustration.

The retail cost of the goal might have been $90, but the wholesale cost was only about half of that. So, for $45, the manager prevented an Internet Boogeyman from coming to life.

We understand that some customers can behave badly. There are some that lie and try to take advantage of businesses, but we happen to believe that people like that are the rare exceptions rather than the rule. We happen to believe you should give them the benefit of the doubt. Cut your losses and move on!

Malcontents and Scoundrels

Some people can never be satisfied. Some may blatantly try to scam/extort/hold your business hostage to their threats. You might even have to deal with schmucks who have nothing better to do with their time and want to try and ruin you because they think it will be fun.

What do you do with people like that? You have options, and some are better than others.

If you run across malcontents and, despite your best efforts, you determine that NOTHING will satisfy them (some may even tell you that there is nothing you can do to make them happy), we encourage you to be responsive in the online forums, social media posts and review sites. Be TRANSPARENT.

Stick to the facts. Be polite. Avoid temptations to engage in name calling no matter how hard they try and bait you. If you make a genuine attempt to help them and do what you say you will do (publicly online, then in the court of public opinion), that may be all you need to do to expose the "haters" for who they really are. It won't look good for them. You may even acquire some sympathy and fans based on how you respond.

Nobody is perfect, and most people understand that. Businesses are run by people who hire people who make mistakes. How a business owner or manager deals with those mistakes can make or break their reputation online.

If a knucklehead employee mistreats a customer and he was in the wrong, the customer may be more likely to ask "What's wrong with this company?" than he is to ask, "What's wrong with that employee?" Why? Because, to the customer, this knucklehead employee IS the company.

Revenge-seeking Internet Boogeymen like to go after the owner or person in charge because they expect the pressure (and consequences) to rain down from above onto the knucklehead employee they have a problem with. If it is warranted, it might be a good idea if the person in charge does in fact hold that employee accountable (re-trains, punishes and/or fires them).

Why? Because, when a situation is fairly investigated and handled transparently online, it shows the public that an owner or manager listens to complaints, looks for solutions to problems, and doesn't duck the responsibility or actions necessary to make things right or better.

If you REALLY get stuck with an Internet Boogeyman who puts out a harmful piece of content, you may be tempted to sue in a real court of law. You could be TOTALLY justified too. And you could TOTALLY be on the right side of the issue and still lose in at least FIVE different ways.

First, if you sue them, don't be surprised if the media picks up on it. As a result, the number of people who actually see it will be significantly greater than if you left things alone and applied the other principles, strategies and tactics we've discussed in this book.

Second, because most media sites are considered highly trusted authority sites, the backlinks they generate to the Internet Boogeyman's content will only drive it higher into major search engines and make it much more difficult (if not impossible) to bury or suppress later on. As if the additional backlinks from the media sites weren't harmful enough, wait until the story starts getting discussed and linked to by bloggers and members of your community on their social media accounts.

Third, even if you "won" in court, you can't get blood out of a turnip. How much are you going to get IF you're even able to collect?

Fourth, just because a court finds in your favor, it's important to remember that there is no Internet erase button. All the stories, links, discussions and social media posts discussing this matter will live on long after it is "settled" in court.

Fifth, it doesn't even take a good Internet Boogeyman to play the victim card even if they are the instigator. After all, in the view of the public, THEY are the ones getting sued by the big, bad business.

Trying to sue an Internet Boogeyman is like trying to put out a fire using gasoline. Alternatively, we encourage you to apply what we've discussed in this book to promote more of your original content created the right way (using keywords in enough of the right places so that it drives the work of the "hater" down into search engine oblivion).

Chapter 7 - The Hardest Cases

As we said from the beginning, most of the ideas and strategies in this book (if implemented correctly and consistently from the beginning) should be capable of helping 95 to 99% of people or business owners with their Internet Boogeyman problems. But what about the hardest of the hardcore cases? Why didn't we talk about them?

There are several reasons.

First, we tried not to make this book overly technical in nature. The complexity of dealing with severe cases goes far beyond what's possible in a casual "non-technical" conversation.

Second, we realize that some people who are (or want to become) Internet Boogeyman might read this book, and we didn't want to give them ideas on how to do a lot of things they didn't already know how to do.

Third, if a person or business is being tormented by those who know what they are doing, then they might be better off reaching out to us and our network of peers for professional assistance instead of trying to handle it their own.

Finally, the cost of dealing with severe cases may involve technical teams, public relations' teams, specialized attorneys and a large budget. For some businesses, it might be better to change their name and re-brand.

We sincerely hope the ideas, strategies and tools we shared make a difference and invite you to send us your success stories.

If you or anyone you know needs assistance beyond what it written about in this book or need an expert keynote speaker for a trade show, conference or special event, please don't hesitate to reach out and let us know. In the meantime, we invite you to connect with us on social media!

About the Authors

Mason Duchatschek

Mason Duchatschek is an online marketing strategist and entrepreneur who helps business owners attract, capture, and convert more of their ideal prospects into customers both online and offline, even if they find web and social media marketing options overwhelming.

As a true "multi-preneur," Mason heads the companies AMO-Employer Services, Inc. (see http://www.ReverseRiskConsulting.com) and Buildatribe, LLC, (see http://www.Buildatribe.com and http://www.BusinessWebVideos.com), which have helped over 1,000 companies maximize the capabilities of social media and web marketing technologies and the people who implement them. He has provided consulting, speaking and thought leadership to major corporations such as Land O'Lakes, Miller Brewing and Purina Mills.

Over the last 20 years, he has coauthored the books *Sales Utopia: How to Get the Right People, Doing the Right Things, Enough Times* with Allen Minster and *Attract, Capture & Convert: 89 Simple Ways Entrepreneurs Make Money Online (& Offline) Using Social Media & Web Marketing Strategy* with Adam Burns and Adam Kreitman.

His ideas have been featured in *Selling Power, Entrepreneur Magazine, The New York Times*, and Fox News.

Adam Burns

Adam Burns started out working part-time at minimum wage for a local sporting goods store 20 years ago and worked his way up to the position of chief operating officer of an eight-location family-owned regional sporting goods chain operating in three states with over 300 employees. Burns has invested countless 14 to 18 hour days working alongside his mentor Mason Duchatschek, exploring and testing strategies related to various marketing efforts such as Facebook, Pinterest, YouTube, Twitter, blog, podcasting, article marketing and more. Burns was asked by Mason to contribute his perspective and experiences to this book.

Will Hanke

Will Hanke is the Chief Search Marketing Strategist at Red Canoe Media (http://redcanoemedia.com), a top St. Louis Search Marketing & SEO firm. In addition to helping some recognizable brands with their online marketing strategy, Will is also an Amazon bestselling author, speaker and teacher. He has also created several online SEO-related video courses for small business owners including his most popular SEO for WordPress series (http://www.SEOmyWordPressWebsite.com/)

Appendix A - Secret Weapons and Valuable Links

Secret Weapon #1 - Distributing content manually takes a long time. Here's an alternative that helps you do it automatically:

Here's our affiliate link. They pay us a referral fee (without raising the cost to you), but we would recommend this service even if they didn't.

www1.instantcustomer.com/cmd.php?af=75353

Secret Weapon #2 - Want to AUTOMATICALLY introduce your YouTube video content to hundreds of active users every day who have interests similar to your areas of expertise?

It can help you EARN more views, likes and shares.

Here's the affiliate link (yes, they pay us a referral fee): https://www.tubeassist.com/?a=TA222

Secret Weapon #3 - What's our favorite keyword research tool? Find out for yourself.

Here's the affiliate link (yes, they pay us a referral fee): http://www.marketsamurai.com/c/buildatribe

Secret Weapon #4 - Get Professional HD (High Definition) Videos Produced for 90 to 95% Less Than Other Top Studios

1. Upload a script.
2. Pick a spokesperson/model.
3. Tell us what text you want on the screen. (Add callouts.)

Then get an HD video you can use for your online marketing for significantly less than other high-end video studios charge!

http://www.BusinessWebVideos.com

Secret Weapon #5 – Get 19 step-by step videos on how to optimize your WordPress website.

If you have a WordPress website, getting it optimized for Google can be a daunting task. Will Hanke's 19 part video series takes the guesswork out of what to click and what to change. Work on your site at your pace, in your own time!

http://www.SEOmyWordPressWebsite.com

Appendix B - Related Books by Mason Duchatschek and Adam Burns

Attract, Capture & Convert: 89 Simple Ways Entrepreneurs Make Money Online (& Offline) Using Social Media and Web Marketing Strategy

See http://www.AttractCaptureConvertBook.com

"This book is filled with money-making information. It is a road map for anyone wanting to become THE recognized expert, market leader or rock star in their industry. Even if all you do is implement one of the 89 ideas in this book, your payoff will be exponential."

- Shep Hyken, New York Times best-selling author, president of the National Speakers Association 2014-2015

"If you want sterile, academic marketing ideas, keep moving. "Attract, Capture and Convert" gives you smart strategies that work in the real world. Chock full of ideas that don't require a huge marketing budget, I guarantee you'll walk away with at least a handful of ideas you want to test in your own business."

-Kathryn Aragon, Blog Editor, The Daily Egg

"If it weren't for this book, I would have made a $17,000 mistake -- and wouldn't have even known it! It's a virtual gold mine of ideas for non-techies who want to establish themselves as an industry authority and increase the demand fro what they do and know!"

-Nancy Bauman, aka "The Book Professor" and Founder of Bookarma.net

Appendix C - Related Books by Will Hanke

How to Set Up Google Authorship for Your WordPress Website

See http://www.amazon.com/author/willhanke

"Big thanks to Will for making this timely resource available. I was able to download the ebook, and implement the step-by-step instructions successfully in just a few minutes. Super easy to follow. Without this guide, I wouldn't have had a clue. With it, getting my site updated was a piece of cake."

- Josh Turner, LinkedSelling.com

"Almost all bloggers have an interest in gaining more traffic through SEO, and Google Authorship is an important piece of that puzzle. Will Hanke helps Wordpress bloggers leverage this

important tool in this exceptional step-by-step guide. I would certainly recommend this e-book to any blogger."

-Ashlyn Brewer, St Louis Social Media Club

Social Media List

Need a professional speaker for an event, meeting or conference?

Contact Mason Duchatschek
mason@buildatribe.com

Contact Will Hanke
will@redcanoemedia.com

For additional tips, strategies and tools, follow visit the following sites and follow us on social media.

Websites:

http://www.Buildatribe.com
http://www.BusinessWebVideos.com
http://www.RedCanoeMedia.com

Social Media:

Twitter:
http://www.Twitter.com/BuildTribes
http://www.Twitter.com/RedCanoeMedia

YouTube:
http://www.YouTube.com/Buildatribe
http://www.YouTube.com/BusinessWebVideos

Facebook:
http://www.Facebook.com/Buildatribe
http://www.Facebook.com/RedCanoeMedia

Pinterest:
http://www.Pinterest.com/Buildatribe

Special Offer Sites: (See the SPECIAL BONUS that is waiting for you!)

http://www.AttractCaptureConvertBook.com
http://www.InternetBoogeymanBook.com
http://www.SEOmyWordPressWebsite.com

Made in the USA
San Bernardino, CA
21 November 2014